Chicken Emotions

by

Normand Leclair

DEDICATED TO:

The many thousands of customers I've had the pleasure of serving.

All the staff who have been and are now part of my wonderful restaurant world.

My sister Terry, with a special thanks for being in my kitchens since 1961.

Illustrations and calligraphy
by
Elizabeth Donovan

Acknowledgements

Mr. Marty Funke,
Mr. and Mrs. Joseph Martella, Sr.,
Ruth Quarnstrom,
Betsy Steinman and Faith Vogt,
of Campus at Lafayette
and J.W. Paquin
have my thanks for their efforts on behalf
of this project.

Published by
DOME PUBLISHING CO., INC.
DOME BUILDING, WARWICK, R. I. 02886

TABLE OF CONTENTS

INTRODUCTION

After starting my cooking career at the age of sixteen, I opened my first restaurant at twenty-five and for the past nineteen years have owned and operated the Red Rooster Tavern in North Kingstown, Rhode Island. It is not an unusual night when we prepare and serve 250 meals. Having people enjoy a dinner gives me great pleasure.

Restaurant dining is not the same thing as home cooking and the offering of a lovely meal prepared for a warm gathering of friends or family is a special gift. Too often the host(ess) is overwhelmed with tedious preparations or elaborate menus requiring them to disappear into the kitchen.

With this collection of recipes, that problem has been solved. These dishes are festive, delicious and easy to prepare. They can be pre-assembled, ready to be whisked into the oven, and baked with no further attention. You can then delight your guests with wonderful food and share the evening with them too.

Enjoy the delightful taste of these dishes and their ease of preparation. May they make both your time spent in the kitchen and the time spent with your guests a pleasure.

Normand Leclair

HINTS AND SUGGESTIONS

All of these recipes are written for two – double or triple the ingredients for more.

To flatten chicken, press between plastic wrap or wax paper with bottom of fry pan.

If you prepare chicken recipes ahead, take them out of the refrigerator 45 minutes before cooking time.

You can substitute margarine for butter.

To make flavored bread crumbs, use 3/4 cups flavored bread crumbs and 1/4 cup corn meal, add paprika for color.

Salt is not used in any of these recipes, herbs and the flavored bread crumbs do the job.

Don't use stainless steel for oven-proof pans. Stainless steel cooks unevenly - use glass or aluminum. *Don't leave chicken overnight in or on aluminum.*

In recipes using patty shells, roll an extra patty shell and decorate chicken package after using the egg wash. I like decorating with my guests' initials, flowers or creative designs.

Boneless chicken can be purchased already prepared at any supermarket.

All recipes are baked in the oven. Oven baked rice, roasted red potatoes, or baked acorn squash, as well as many other vegetable dishes can be prepared in the oven at the same time. Steaming vegetables is another very quick way to cook them.

On spices: "Accentuate, don't overtake" is a good rule to follow. All recipes are lightly spiced.

A full flavored white wine such as a Chablis or Chardonnay will compliment these dishes without overwhelming them.

Use a spatula to remove chicken from the pan so portions don't break or fall apart.

The word *reserve,* found in some of the following recipes, means "to put aside", to be used later in assembling the dinners.

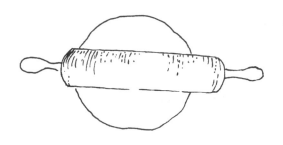

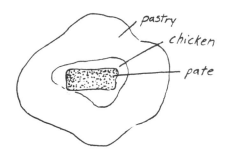

pastry

chicken

pate

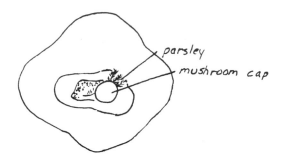

parsley

mushroom cap

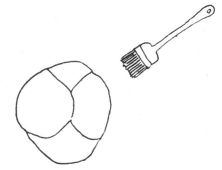

2 whole chicken breasts, skinned, boned, halved and
    flattened with excess fat removed
2 Pepperidge Farm Patty Shells, thawed, (available
    at most markets)
1 small can of pâté or fresh pâté from a specialty market
Sprig of chopped parsley
1/2 cup flavored bread crumbs
2 teaspoons olive oil
2 teaspoons water
Flour for rolling patty shells
1 egg
1/2 teaspoon milk

PREPARATION
1. In a flat dish, press crumbs into chicken on both sides.
2. In a sauté pan using half the oil, lightly sauté the breaded chicken breasts; reserve and cool.
3. On a floured board, roll thawed patty shells about 8x8 round; reserve and keep cool.

ASSEMBLY
1. On a flat surface, lay out pastry. Top successively with one cooked chicken breast, slice of pâté, other chicken breast. Add more pâté and parsley. Top with mushroom cap.
2. Do this with each portion.
3. Wrap chicken like a package, sealing seams with water.
4. In a cup, beat egg and milk with a fork.
5. Spread egg mixture on crust with fingers or pastry brush.
6. Put chicken on oiled and floured cookie sheet.
7. Bake on top shelf of preheated 400° oven for 20 minutes.
8. Remove from oven with a spatula. Serve on heated plates.

1 whole chicken breast, skinned, boned,
    halved and flattened with excess fat removed
2 Pepperidge Farm Patty Shells, thawed (available
    at most markets)
1/2 cup flavored bread crumbs
1 cup tomato sauce
Sprig of fresh parsley, chopped
2 teaspoons olive oil
 Flour for rolling pastry
1/4 teaspoon basil
2 slices of provolone cheese

PREPARATION
1. In a flat dish, press bread crumbs into chicken on both sides; reserve.
2. On a floured board, roll thawed patty shells about 8x8 round; reserve and keep cool.

ASSEMBLY
1. Oil and flour a small cookie sheet or oven-proof casserole dish.
2. Lay out pastry. Put breaded chicken in center and crimp pastry around chicken, higher than chicken.
3. Put chicken pastry on cookie sheet.. Spread with tomato sauce. Top with basil and provolone cheese and garnish with chopped parsley.
4. Bake in a preheated 400° oven for 25 minutes.
5. Remove from oven with a spatula, serve on heated plates.

FOR VARIATIONS, USE TOPPINGS THAT ARE USED ON PIZZA.

CHICKEN BREAST BAKED IN A CRUST WITH HAM AND SWISS CHEESE

2 whole chicken breasts, skinned, boned, halved and
    flattened with excess fat removed
2 Pepperidge Farm Patty Shells, thawed (available at
    most markets)
2 slices of ham
2 slices Swiss cheese
2 large mushroom caps without stems
Sprig of fresh chopped parsley
1 egg
1/2 teaspoon milk
1/2 cup flavored bread crumbs
2 teaspoons olive oil

PREPARATION
1. In a flat dish, press bread crumbs into chicken on both sides.
2. In a sauté pan using half the oil, lightly sauté the breaded chicken breasts; reserve and cool.
3. On a floured board, roll thawed patty shells about 8x8 round; reserve and keep cool.

ASSEMBLY
1. On a flat surface, lay out pastry. Top successively with one cooked chicken breast, slice of ham, other chicken breast, Swiss cheese, mushroom cap and parsley.
2. Do this with each portion.
3. Wrap chicken like a package, sealing seams with water.
4. In a cup, beat egg and milk with fork.
5. Spread egg mixture on crust with fingers or pastry brush.
6. Put chicken package on oiled and floured cookie sheet.
7. Bake on top shelf of a preheated 400° oven for 20 minutes.
8. Remove from oven with a spatula, serve on heated plates.

2 whole chicken breasts, skinned, boned, halved and
 flattened with excess fat removed
1/2 cup flavored bread crumbs
2 teaspoons olive oil
1/2 cup chopped watercress
2 large cloves chopped garlic
1/2 cup cream cheese
2 Pepperidge Farm Patty Shells (available at most
 markets)
2 large mushrooms without stems
1 egg
1/2 teaspoon milk
2 teaspoons water

PREPARATION
1. In a flat dish, press crumbs into chicken on both sides.
2. In a sauté pan using half the oil, lightly sauté the breaded chicken breasts; reserve and cool.
3. On a floured board, roll thawed patty shells about 8x8 round; reserve and keep cool.
4. In a mixing bowl, mix watercress, chopped garlic and cream cheese until smooth; reserve.
5. Oil and flour a cookie sheet for baking.

ASSEMBLY
1. On a flat surface, lay out pastry. Top successively with one cooked chicken breast, cream cheese mixture, other chicken breast. Top with mushroom cap.
2. Do this with each portion.
3. Wrap chicken like a package, sealing seams with water.
4. In a cup, beat egg and milk with a fork.
5. Spread egg mixture on crust with fingers or pastry brush.
6. Put chicken package on oiled and floured cookie sheet.
7. Bake on top shelf of a preheated 400° oven for 20 minutes.
8. Remove from oven with a spatula, serve on heated plates.

CHICKEN SYLVIA

2 whole chicken breasts, skinned, boned, halved and
    flattened with excess fat removed
2 Pepperidge Farm Shells, thawed (available at most
    markets)
2 teaspoons water
2 slices ham
2 slices Swiss cheese
1 apple, peeled, cored, quartered
1 oz. butter
1/2 cup flavored bread crumbs
2 teaspoons olive oil
Flour for rolling pastry
Touch nutmeg
1 egg
1/2 teaspoon milk

PREPARATION
1. In a flat dish, press bread crumbs into chicken on both sides.
2. In a sauté pan using half the oil, lightly sauté the breaded
   chicken breasts; cool and reserve.
3. On a floured board, roll thawed patty shells about 8x8 round;
   reserve and keep cool.
4. Oil and flour a cookie sheet.

ASSEMBLY
1. On a flat surface, lay out pastry. Top successively with one
   cooked chicken breast, slice of ham, other chicken breast, Swiss
   cheese, half apple, dash of nutmeg and dot with butter.
2. Wrap chicken like a package, sealing seams with water.
3. Do this with each portion.
4. In a cup, beat egg and milk with fork.
5. Spread egg mixture on crust with fingers or pastry brush.
6. Put chicken package on oiled and floured cookie sheet.
7. Bake on the top shelf of a preheated 400° oven for 20 minutes.
8. Remove from oven with a spatula. Serve on heated plates.

WINE, FIREPLACE, AND CANDLELIGHT WILL MAKE THIS
DINNER PERFECT.

OVEN POACHED CHICKEN WITH VEGETABLES

2 whole chicken breasts, skinned, boned, halved and
   flattened with excess fat removed
1 small carrot, peeled, cut like match sticks
2 small onions, peeled, cut in half
1 small zucchini cut in quarters
4 cleaned mushroom caps without stems
4 cherry tomatoes or 2 small tomatoes cut in half
1/2 teaspoon tarragon
1/2 cup flour
1 cup white wine or chicken stock

PREPARATION

1. This dish needs a casserole with a cover that can contain the four pieces of chicken and the vegetables.
2. In a flat dish, press chicken in flour on both sides; reserve.

ASSEMBLY

1. Lay floured chicken breasts in the casserole dish. Around the chicken add all the prepared vegetables, carrots, onions, tomatoes, mushrooms, and zucchini.
2. Sprinkle with tarragon.
3. Add wine or chicken stock.
4. Cover the casserole dish and bake in a preheated 400° oven for 20 minutes.
5. Remove from oven. With a large spoon, remove chicken to heated plates. Spoon on the vegetables and wine sauce. The sauce will thicken because of the flour.

LEMON CHICKEN

2 whole chicken breasts, skinned, boned, halved and
    flattened with excess fat removed
1/2 cup flour
1 cup chicken stock
2 teaspoons lemon juice
 Sprig of chopped parsley
1 small onion chopped
2 teaspoons butter

PREPARATION
1. In a flat dish, press the chicken in flour on both sides; reserve.
2. In a small bowl combine chicken broth, lemon juice, chopped parsley, chopped onion; reserve.
3. Oven-proof casserole dish large enough to contain 4 chicken breasts.

ASSEMBLY
1. Lay out floured chicken breasts in oven-proof casserole.
2. Add lemon mixture to chicken, dot with butter.
3. Bake in a preheated 400° oven for 20 minutes.
4. Remove chicken from oven to heated plates, spoon remaining sauce on chicken.

THIS DISH GOES WELL WITH RICE.

2 whole chicken breasts, skinned, boned, halved
   and flattened with excess fat removed
1/2 cup flavored bread crumbs
4 mushroom caps, stems removed
2 teaspoons butter
   GLAZE:
1/2 cup apricot jelly
2 garlic cloves, minced
1/8 teaspoon ginger
 Pinch of crushed red pepper
1 tablespoon white vinegar
1 tablespoon soy sauce

PREPARATION

1. In a flat dish, press crumbs into chicken on both sides; reserve.
2. Mix well in a bowl, apricot jelly, chopped garlic, ginger, red pepper, vinegar, soy sauce and chopped parsley; reserve.
3. Using half the butter, butter one oven-proof casserole dish large enough to contain the four chicken breasts.

ASSEMBLY

1. Lay out chicken in casserole dish. Top with mushroom caps. Spoon apricot glaze on chicken and mushrooms and dot with remaining butter.
2. Bake in a preheated 400° oven for 20 minutes.
3. Remove chicken to heated serving plates and spoon remaining glaze on chicken.

ORANGE CHICKEN

2 whole chicken breasts, skinned, boned, halved and
   flattened with excess fat removed
2 oranges, peeled and sliced with seeds removed
1/2 cup flavored bread crumbs
2 teaspoons butter
1 cup orange juice
1 teaspoon soy sauce
1/4 teaspoon ginger
1/4 teaspoon allspice
2 teaspoons brown sugar
Sprig of fresh chopped parsley

PREPARATION
1. In a flat dish, press crumbs into chicken on both sides;
   reserve.
2. In a bowl, add orange juice, soy sauce, ginger, allspice and
   brown sugar. Mix well; reserve.
3. Using half the butter, butter one oven-proof casserole dish
   large enough to contain the four chicken breasts.

ASSEMBLY
1. Lay out chicken in casserole dish. Put orange slices on chicken
   and add orange juice mixture on and around chicken. Garnish
   with parsley and dot with butter.
2. Bake in a preheated 400° oven for 20 minutes.
3. Remove chicken from casserole to heated plates and spoon
   remaining sauce on chicken.

TOMATO CHEESE CHICKEN

2 whole chicken breasts, skinned, boned, halved and
  flattened with excess fat removed
2 tomatoes, sliced
4 slices provolone cheese
1/4 teaspoon dried basil or fresh basil leaves
Sprig of fresh chopped parsley
2 teaspoons olive oil
1/2 cup of flavored bread crumbs

PREPARATION
1. In a flat dish, press crumbs into chicken on both sides; reserve.
2. Oil one oven-proof casserole dish large enough to contain the
   four breaded chicken breasts.

ASSEMBLY
1. Lay out chicken in oiled casserole. Top chicken with tomato
   slices. Sprinkle tomato slices with basil or basil leaves. Top
   with provolone cheese and garnish with chopped parsley.
2. Bake in a preheated 400° oven for 20 minutes.
3. Remove from oven with a spatula. Serve on heated plates.

THIS IS A GREAT DISH WHEN NATIVE TOMATOES ARE IN SEASON.

2 whole chicken breasts, skinned, boned,
   halved and flattened with excess fat removed
1/2 cup flavored bread crumbs
2 teaspoons butter
Sprig of chopped parsley
1 cup sour cream
4 ounces blue cheese
1/2 teaspoon Worcestershire sauce
2 cloves chopped garlic
Dash of paprika

PREPARATION

1. In a flat dish, press bread crumbs into chicken on both sides; reserve.
2. In a mixing bowl, add blue cheese. Crumble with a fork. Add sour cream, chopped garlic, Worcestershire sauce and chopped parsley. Mix well; reserve.
3. Butter an oven-proof casserole dish large enough to contain the four chicken breasts.

ASSEMBLY

1. Lay the breaded chicken in buttered casserole dish. Spoon cheese mixture on each chicken breast. Sprinkle with paprika.
2. Bake in a preheated 400° oven for 20 minutes.
3. Remove from oven to heated plates. Spoon remaining sauce on and around chicken.

SPICY, NEEDS SIMPLE VEGETABLES.

CHICKEN WITH WHITE GRAPES

2 whole chicken breasts, skinned, boned, halved
and flattened with excess fat removed
1 cup seedless white grapes without stems
1 cup white wine or chicken stock
2 teaspoons butter
Sprig of fresh parsley, chopped
1/2 cup flavored bread crumbs

PREPARATION
1. In a flat dish, press crumbs into chicken on both sides; reserve.
2. Using half the butter, butter one oven-proof casserole dish large
   enough to contain the four chicken breasts.

ASSEMBLY
1. Lay breaded chicken in casserole dish. Add seedless grapes,
   white wine or chicken stock. Dot with butter and garnish with
   parsley.
2. Bake in a preheated 400° oven for 20 minutes.
3. Remove to heated plates. Spoon grapes and sauce on and around
   chicken.

CHICKEN INDIENNE

2 whole chicken breasts, skinned, boned, halved and
    flattened with excess fat removed
1/2 cup flavored bread crumbs
1 small jar Mango Chutney
1/2 cup sliced almonds
1/4 teaspoon curry powder
2 teaspoons olive oil
2 teaspoons butter
Sprig of chopped parsley

PREPARATION
1. In a flat dish, press crumbs into chicken on both sides; reserve.
2. Oil one oven-proof casserole dish large enough to contain the four chicken breasts.

ASSEMBLY
1. Lay chicken in casserole dish. Spoon chutney on chicken and sprinkle with curry. Top with almonds and parsley and dot with butter.
2. Bake in a preheated 400° oven for 20 minutes.
3. Remove to heated plates with spatula. Enjoy the great aroma.

ITALIAN SAUSAGE CHICKEN LORRAINE

2 whole chicken breasts, skinned, boned, halved and
    flattened with excess fat removed
1 cup tomato sauce, (marinara sauce)
4 cooked Italian sausages, hot or sweet, cut in half
    lengthwise
1/2 cup flavored bread crumbs
2 teaspoons olive oil
4 slices provolone cheese
Sprig of fresh, chopped parsley

PREPARATION
1. In a flat dish, press bread crumbs into chicken on both sides;
   reserve.
2. Oil one oven-proof casserole dish large enough to contain the
   four chicken breasts.

ASSEMBLY
1. Lay chicken in oiled casserole dish. Top with split sausage.
   Spoon tomato sauce between sausage. Top with provolone
   cheese and chopped parsley.
2. Bake in a preheated 400° oven for 20 minutes.
3. Remove from oven with a spatula to heated plates. Spoon remaining sauce around chicken.

HERE IS ANOTHER GOOD WAY TO USE LEFTOVER TOMATO SAUCE.

MUSTARD PECAN CHICKEN

2 whole chicken breasts, skinned, boned, halved and
    flattened with excess fat removed
1/2 cup flavored bread crumbs
1 cup whole egg mayonnaise
2 teaspoons whole grain mustard
1/2 cup chopped pecans
2 teaspoons olive oil
Sprig of chopped parsley

PREPARATION
1. In a flat dish, press bread crumbs into chicken on both sides;
   reserve.
2. In a mixing bowl, mix mustard and mayonnaise well; reserve.
3. Oil an oven-proof casserole dish large enough to contain the
   four chicken breasts.

ASSEMBLY
1. Lay the breaded chicken in casserole dish. With a spoon, spread
   mustard mixture on chicken evenly. Top with chopped pecans
   and garnish with parsley.
2. Bake in a preheated 400° oven for 20 minutes.
3. Remove from oven with a spatula. Serve on heated plates.

ALMOND CHICKEN

2 whole chicken breasts, skinned, boned, halved and
   flattened with excess fat removed
1/2 cup flavored bread crumbs
1/2 cup sliced almonds
2 teaspoons butter
2 teaspoons olive oil
Sprig of fresh chopped parsley

PREPARATION
1. In a flat dish, press bread crumbs into chicken on both sides;
   reserve.
2. Oil an oven-proof casserole dish large enough to contain the
   four chicken breasts.

ASSEMBLY
1. Lay the breaded chicken breasts in oiled casserole dish. Top
   with almonds and parsley and dot with butter.
2. Bake in a preheated 400° oven for 20 minutes.
3. Remove chicken to heated plates with spatula.

CHICKEN HAWAIIAN ─────────

2 whole chicken breasts, skinned, boned, halved and
    flattened with excess fat removed
4 canned pineapple rings (reserve juice)
4 slices ham
4 slices Monterey Jack cheese
 Sprig of chopped parsley
1/2 cup flavored bread crumbs
1/2 cup butter

PREPARATION
1. In a flat dish, press bread crumbs into chicken on both sides;
   reserve.
2. An oven-proof casserole dish large enough to contain two
   chicken breasts.

ASSEMBLY
1. Lay two chicken breast halves side by side in casserole dish.
   Top successively with slice of ham, chicken half, pineapple,
   Monterey Jack cheese, parsley and butter.
2. Add pineapple juice to casserole.
3.Bake in a preheated 400° oven for 25 minutes.
4. Remove from oven and serve on heated plates.
5. Spoon remaining juices around chicken.

SESAME CHICKEN

2 whole chicken breasts, skinned, boned, halved and
    flattened with excess fat removed
1 cup sesame seeds
2 teaspoons butter
2 teaspoons olive oil
Sprig of fresh parsley chopped

PREPARATION
1. In a flat dish, press sesame seeds and parsley into chicken on both sides; reserve.
2. Oil an oven-proof casserole dish large enough to contain the four chicken breasts.

ASSEMBLY
1. Lay the prepared chicken breasts in oiled casserole dish. Dot with butter.
2. Bake in a preheated 400° oven for 20 minutes.
3. Remove chicken to heated plates with spatula.

VERY MILD, THIS DISH NEEDS SIMPLE VEGETABLES.

2 whole chicken breasts, skinned, boned,
   halved and flattened with excess fat removed
1/2 cup flavored bread crumbs
2 ripe bananas
1/2 cup sliced almonds
1 cup grapefruit juice
1/4 teaspoon curry
2 teaspoons butter
Sprig of fresh chopped parsley

PREPARATION

1. In a flat dish press bread crumbs into chicken on both sides; reserve.
2. Prepare an oven proof casserole dish large enough to contain the four chicken breasts plus bananas.

ASSEMBLY

1. Put chicken and peeled bananas in casserole dish. Top chicken with almonds, curry and butter and add grapefruit juice.
2. Bake in a preheated 400° oven for 20 minutes.
3. Remove chicken from casserole dish to heated plates. Top with bananas. Spoon juice on and around chicken. Garnish with chopped parsley.

CHICKEN IN A CRUST WITH ASPARAGUS AND SWEET RED PEPPER

2 whole chicken breasts, skinned boned, halved and
    flattened with excess fat removed
8 fresh asparagus spears, trimmed, blanched
1 large sweet red pepper
4 slices American cheese
1/4 teaspoon basil
2 teaspoons olive oil
1/2 cup flour for rolling pastry shells
2 Pepperidge Farm Patty Shells, thawed (available at
    most markets)
1 egg
1 teaspoon milk
1/2 cup flavored bread crumbs
2 teaspoons water

PREPARATION
1. In a flat dish, press bread crumbs into chicken on both sides.
2. In a sauté pan using half the oil, lightly sauté the breaded chicken breasts; reserve and cool.
3. On a floured board, roll thawed patty shells about 8x8 round; reserve and cool.
4. Heat broiler. Cut red pepper in four, remove seeds and trim. Brown pepper under broiler lightly. Let cool and peel off skins; reserve and cool.
5. Steam asparagus just one minute, must be firm; reserve and cool.

ASSEMBLY
1. On a flat surface, lay out pastry. Top successively with one cooked chicken breast, four asparagus spears, other chicken breast, half red pepper, pinch basil and 2 slices American cheese.
2. Repeat with each portion
3. Wrap chicken like a package, sealing seams with water.
4. In a cup, beat egg and milk with a fork.
5. Spread egg mixture on crust with fingers or pastry brush.
6. Put chicken package on oiled and floured cookie sheet.
7. Bake on top of shelf of preheated 400° oven for 20 minutes.

CHICKEN FLORENTINE

2 whole chicken breasts, skinned, boned, halved and
   flattened with excess fat removed
1/2 cup flavored bread crumbs
2 teaspoons olive oil
1 package fresh spinach, trimmed and cleaned
1 small chopped onion
2 teaspoons butter
4 thin slices of cheddar cheese
1/8 teaspoon nutmeg
Sprig of chopped parsley

PREPARATION
1. In a flat dish, press bread crumbs into chicken on both
   sides, reserve.
2. In a sauté pan, sauté chopped onion in butter until yellow. Add spinach and nutmeg. Cook until wilted; reserve
   and cool.
3. Oil an oven-proof casserole dish large enough to contain
   the four chicken breasts.

ASSEMBLY
1. Lay breaded chicken in oiled casserole dish. Spoon
   spinach mixture on each chicken breast. Top with cheddar cheese and chopped parsley.
2. Bake in a preheated 400° oven for 20 minutes.
3. Remove from oven with a spatula. Serve on heated
   plates.

HERE IS A BEAUTIFUL BLEND OF SPINACH AND CHEESE.

CRABMEAT CHICKEN ════════

2 whole chicken breasts, skinned, boned, halved and
    flattened with excess fat removed
1/2 cup flavored bread crumbs
4 mushroom caps without stems
4 ounces crabmeat, cleaned
Sprig of chopped, fresh dill or 1/2 teaspoon dried dill
4 slices Monterey Jack cheese
2 teaspoons butter
2 teaspoons olive oil

PREPARATION
1. In a flat dish, press bread crumbs into chicken on both sides; reserve.
2. Oil an oven-proof casserole dish large enough to contain the four chicken breasts.
3. In a small mixing bowl, mix crabmeat and dill; reserve.

ASSEMBLY
1. Lay breaded chicken in oiled casserole dish. On each chicken breast add crabmeat and mushroom cap. Dot with butter and top with Monterey Jack cheese.
2. Bake in a preheated 400° oven for 20 minutes.
3. Remove from oven with a spatula. Serve on heated plates.

CHICKEN ROCKEFELLER

2 whole chicken breasts, skinned, boned, halved and
   flattened with excess fat removed
1/2 cup flavored bread crumbs
2 teaspoons olive oil
1 package fresh spinach, trimmed and cleaned
1 small chopped onion
2 teaspoons butter
1 teaspoon Pernod Liquor
4 slices Monterey Jack cheese
Sprig of fresh chopped parsley

PREPARATION
1. In a flat dish, press bread crumbs into chicken on both sides;
   reserve.
2. Add butter to a sauté pan. Sauté onion until yellow. Add spinach
   and Pernod Liquor and cook until wilted; reserve and cool.
3. Oil an oven-proof casserole dish large enough to contain the
   four chicken breasts.

ASSEMBLY
1. Lay chicken in oiled casserole dish. Spoon spinach mixture on
   each breast. Top with Monterey Jack cheese and garnish with
   chopped parsley.
2. Bake in a preheated 400° oven for 20 minutes.
3. Remove from oven with a spatula. Serve on heated plates.

PERNOD, SPINACH AND CHEESE GO SO WELL TOGETHER.

As for rosemary,
I let it run
all over my garden walls,
not only because
my bees love it
but because it is
the herb sacred
to remembrance
and to friendship,
whence a sprig of it
hath a
dumb language.

Sir Thomas More

ROSEMARY ALMOND CHICKEN

2 whole chicken breasts, skinned, boned, halved and
    flattened with excess fat removed
1 small onion, chopped
1 teaspoon dried or fresh rosemary
1 10 1/2 oz can condensed cream of celery soup
1/2 cup light cream
1/2 teaspoon poultry seasoning
1/2 cup flavored bread crumbs
1/4 cup sliced almonds
2 teaspoons butter
Sprig of chopped parsley

PREPARATION
1. In a flat dish, press bread crumbs into chicken on both sides; reserve.
2. In a bowl, add cream of celery soup, cream, poultry seasoning, rosemary, parsley and chopped onion. Mix well; reserve.
3. One oven-proof casserole dish large enough to contain the four chicken breasts.

ASSEMBLY
1. Lay out chicken breasts in oven-proof casserole dish.
2. Spoon soup mixture around chicken.
3. Sprinkle with almonds. Dot with butter.
4. Bake in a preheated 400° oven for 20 minutes.
5. Remove chicken from casserole dish to heated serving plates. Spoon sauce on and around chicken.

CHEDDAR CHICKEN ═══════════

2 whole chicken breasts, skinned, boned, halved and
    flattened with excess fat removed
4 slices bacon cooked and chopped
1/2 cup sweet and sour sauce (available at super-
    market)
1/2 pound chopped, sharp cheddar
1/2 cup green onions, chopped, white and green parts
2 teaspoons olive oil
2 teaspoons butter
1/2 cup flavored bread crumbs
1 apple, peeled, cored, chopped

PREPARATION
1. In a flat dish, press bread crumbs into chicken on both sides;
   reserve.
2. In a mixing bowl, combine chopped bacon, sweet and sour
   sauce, grated cheddar, green onions and chopped apple. Mix
   well; reserve.
3. Oil an oven-proof casserole dish large enough to contain the
   four chicken breasts.

ASSEMBLY
1. Lay the breaded chicken breasts in oiled casserole dish. Spoon
   cheddar mixture on each breast. Dot with butter.
2. Bake in a preheated 400° oven for 20 minutes.
3. Remove from oven to heated plates with a spatula. Spoon any
   mixture left in casserole on chicken.

HAZELNUT CHICKEN WITH FRESH PEACHES AND FRANGELICO

2 whole chicken breasts, skinned, boned, halved and
    flattened with excess fat removed
1 cup chopped hazelnuts
1 ripe peach
1/2 cup cream
2 teaspoons butter
1/4 cup Frangelico
Sprig of chopped parsley

PREPARATION
1. In a flat plate, press chicken into hazelnuts on both sides; reserve.
2. Peel peach and slice; reserve.
3. In a small bowl, mix Frangelico, cream and parsley; reserve.

ASSEMBLY
1. Using half the butter, butter a casserole dish for the four chicken
breasts.
2. Lay the prepared chicken in casserole dish.
3. Add peaches to casserole and dot with butter.
4. Bake in a preheated 400° oven for 20 minutes.
5. Remove from oven, add Frangelico mixture and return to oven
for about 5 minutes.
6. Remove chicken and peaches to heated plates. Spoon sauce on
chicken and peaches.
7. Garnish with chopped parsley.

THIS DISH GOES WELL WITH RICE.

2 whole chicken breasts, skinned, boned, halved and
    flattened with excess fat removed
1/2 cup flavored bread crumbs
2 tablespoons butter
1 small finely chopped onion
1/2 cup cooked rice
1/4 cup white raisins
Sprig chopped parsley
1/2 teaspoon curry powder
1/4 teaspoon poultry seasoning
1/2 teaspoon brown sugar
1 clove chopped garlic
2 teaspoons olive oil
4 slices Monterey Jack cheese

PREPARATION

1. In a flat dish, press bread crumbs into chicken on both sides; reserve.
2. Make stuffing by melting butter in fry pan. Cook onion until yellow. Add garlic, rice, raisins, parsley, curry, poultry seasoning and brown sugar. Mix well; reserve and cool.
3. Oil an oven-proof casserole dish large enough to contain the four chicken breasts.

ASSEMBLY

1. Lay breaded chicken in oiled casserole dish. On each breast, spoon prepared stuffing. Top each portion with Monterey Jack cheese.
2. Bake in a preheated 400° oven for 20 minutes.
3. Remove from oven with a spatula . Serve on heated plates.

RICE, RAISINS, CURRY, AND CHEESE MAKE THIS DISH A SURPRISE.

CHICKEN CASINO ═══════════════

2 whole chicken breasts, skinned, boned, halved and
    flattened with excess fat removed
1 sweet red pepper or yellow pepper
1 small red onion
1/2 cup olive oil
1 teaspoon dried basil
Pinch of fennel seeds
1/2 cup flavored bread crumbs
2 slices bacon

PREPARATION
1. In a flat dish, press bread crumbs into chicken on both sides; reserve.
2. Oil one oven-proof casserole dish large enough to contain the four chicken breasts.
3. Core pepper, cut in quarters, slice thin; reserve.
4. Peel onion, cut in quarters, slice thin; reserve.
5. In a small bowl, add peppers, onions, basil, fennel, half of oil. Mix well; reserve.

ASSEMBLY
1. Place chicken in oiled casserole dish.
2. Place the pepper-onion mixture on each chicken breast.
3. Put 1/2 slice of bacon on each prepared chicken breast.
4. Bake on the top shelf of a preheated 400° oven for 20 minutes.
5. Remove from oven with a spatula. Serve on heated plates.

THIS DISH IS VERY PLEASING TO THE EYE AND WILL MAKE THE
HOUSE SMELL WONDERFUL.

2 whole chicken breasts, skinned, boned, halved and
    flattened with excess fat removed
1 small eggplant, peeled, cut into 1/2 inch slices
1/2 cup flavored bread crumbs
1/2 cup flour 4 slices provolone cheese
1/4 cup grated cheese
1/2 cup tomato sauce, (marinara sauce)
2 teaspoons olive oil
1 teaspoon salt
Sprig of chopped fresh parsley

PREPARATION

1. Salt the slices of eggplant . Let them sit for one hour. Rinse and
   dry with paper towels.
2. Flour the eggplant . Saute the slices on both sides, using half the
   oil. Remove and drain on paper towels; cool and reserve.
3. In a flat dish, press bread crumbs into chicken on both sides;
   reserve.
4. Oil one oven-proof casserole dish large enough to contain the
   four chicken breasts.

ASSEMBLY

1. Lay out chicken in oiled casserole dish.
2. Top each breast with eggplant. Top with tomato sauce, grated
   cheese, then provolone cheese. Garnish with parsley.
3. Bake in a preheated 400° oven for 20 minutes.
4. Remove from casserole with spatula. Serve on heated plates.

The table
attracts more friends
than the mind

Publilius Syrus

CHEESE AND SAUERKRAUT CHICKEN

2 whole chicken breasts, skinned, boned,
    halved and flattened with excess fat removed
1/2 cup flavored bread crumbs
2 teaspoons olive oil
Small can sauerkraut, one cup
4 slices Swiss cheese
Sprig of fresh parsley, chopped
Pinch fennel seeds
1/2 cup Thousand Island dressing

PREPARATION
1. In a flat dish, press bread crumbs into chicken on both sides; reserve.
2. Oil one oven-proof casserole dish large enough to contain the four chicken breasts.

ASSEMBLY
1. Lay chicken in oiled casserole dish.
2. Spread the sauerkraut on top of chicken. Spoon Thousand Island dressing on sauerkraut. Sprinkle fennel seeds. Top with Swiss cheese and sprinkle with parsley.
3. Bake in a preheated 400° oven for 20 minutes.
4. Remove from oven with a spatula. Serve on heated plates.

CHICKEN CORDON BLEU

2 whole chicken breasts, skinned, boned, halved and
    flattened with excess fat removed
4 slices ham (same size as chicken)
4 slices Swiss cheese
1/2 cup flavored bread crumbs
2 teaspoons olive oil
1 cup brown sauce (available at supermarkets)
Sprig of parsley, chopped

PREPARATION
1. In a flat dish, press bread crumbs into chicken on both sides; reserve.
2. Oil an oven-proof casserole dish large enough to contain the four chicken breasts.

ASSEMBLY
1. Lay the four chicken breasts in the oiled casserole dish.
2. Put one slice of ham on top of each breast.
3. Put one slice of Swiss cheese on top of ham.
4. Garnish chicken with parsley.
5. Bake in preheated 400° oven for 20 minutes.
6. Heat brown gravy on low heat until warm. Madeira or Marsala wine can be added.
7. Remove chicken from oven. Spoon sauce on and around chicken. Serve on heated plates.

2 whole chicken breasts, skinned, boned, halved and
    flattened with excess fat removed
1/2 cup flavored bread crumbs
1/2 cup pesto (available in specialty stores)
4 slices provolone cheese
Sprig of chopped parsley
2 teaspoons olive oil

PREPARATION
1. In a flat dish, press bread crumbs into chicken on both sides; reserve.
2. Oil one oven-proof casserole dish large enough to contain the four chicken breasts.

ASSEMBLY
1. Lay chicken in oiled casserole dish.
2. Spoon pesto on chicken. Top with provolone cheese and chopped parsley.
3. Bake in a preheated 400° oven for 20 minutes.
4. Remove to heated plates with spatula.

CHICKEN PARMIGIANA ═══════

2 whole chicken breasts, skinned, boned, halved and
    flattened with excess fat removed
1/2 cup flavored bread crumbs
1 cup tomato sauce
4 slices provolone cheese
2 teaspoons grated cheese
2 teaspoons olive oil
Sprinkle of basil
Sprig of chopped fresh parsley

PREPARATION
1. In a flat dish, press bread crumbs into chicken on both sides;
   reserve.
2. Oil one oven-proof casserole dish large enough to contain the
   four chicken breasts.

ASSEMBLY
1. Lay chicken in oiled casserole dish.
2. Spread tomato sauce on breaded chicken. Sprinkle with basil
   and grated cheese. Top with provolone cheese. Garnish with
   chopped parsley.
3. Bake in a preheated 400° oven for 20 minutes.
4. Remove to heated plates, spoon remaining sauce around
   chicken.

2 whole chicken breasts, skinned, boned,
    halved and flattened with excess fat removed
1 cup smashed corn flakes
2 egg
1/4 cup milk
2 teaspoons butter
2 teaspoons olive oil
1/8 teaspoon thyme

PREPARATION

1. Beat eggs and milk in a small bowl; reserve.
2. Mix smashed corn flakes with thyme. Put on a flat plate; re-serve.
3. Oil a small cookie sheet or oven-proof casserole dish.

ASSEMBLY

1. Dip chicken in egg mixture one at a time, then press in corn-flakes on both sides.
2. Lay out the chicken breasts on oiled cookie sheet.
3. Dot with butter.
4. Bake in a preheated 400° oven for 20 minutes.
5. Remove from oven with a spatula. Serve on heated plates.

SIMPLE BUT ELEGANT.

CHICKEN, BAKED WITH SPINACH, PINE NUTS, PROVOLONE CHEESE

2 whole chicken breasts, skinned, boned, halved and
    flattened with excess fat removed
1 package fresh spinach, trimmed, washed
4 slices provolone cheese
2 teaspoons pine nuts
1 teaspoon grated cheese
1/2 cup flavored bread crumbs
1/2 cup olive oil
2 cloves chopped garlic
Sprig of chopped fresh parsley

PREPARATION
1. In a flat dish, press bread crumbs into chicken on both sides; reserve.
2. In a sauté pan, sauté garlic in half of olive oil just a minute. Add spinach, pine nuts, grated cheese. Sauté until spinach is limp; cool and reserve.
3. Oil one oven-proof casserole dish large enough to contain the four chicken breasts.

ASSEMBLY
1. Lay the four chicken breasts in casserole dish.
2. On each breast spoon spinach mixture. Top with provolone cheese. Garnish with chopped parsley.
3. Bake in a preheated 400° oven for 20 minutes.
4. Remove from casserole with spatula. Serve on heated plates.

2 whole chicken breasts, skinned, boned, halved and
    flattened with excess fat removed
1/2 cup flavored bread crumbs
1 small can of pitted sour cherries in water, reserve
    liquid
1 teaspoon sugar
1/2 teaspoon grated lemon rind
1/8 teaspoon allspice
2 teaspoons butter
1 small finely chopped onion
1/2 cup sliced almonds

PREPARATION
1. In a flat dish, press crumbs into chicken on both sides; reserve.
2. In a mixing bowl, mix cherries, cherry juice, onions, allspice, lemon rind and sugar; reserve.
3. Oven-proof casserole dish large enough to contain the four chicken breasts.

ASSEMBLY
1. Place breaded chicken in casserole dish.
2. Spoon cherry mixture around chicken. Top with sliced almonds and dot with butter.
3. Bake in a preheated 400° oven for 20 minutes.
4. Remove chicken to heated plates. Spoon cherry mixture over and around chicken.

CHICKEN AND SHRIMP COMBINATION

1 whole chicken breast, skinned, boned, halved and
    flattened with excess fat removed
4 large shrimp, cleaned, shelled, and split with tail
    removed
4 asparagus spears, blanched
2 slices Monterey Jack cheese
1 teaspoon butter
2 teaspoons olive oil
Dash of nutmeg
Sprig of chopped parsley
1/2 cup flavored bread crumbs

PREPARATION
1. In a flat dish, press crumbs into chicken on both sides; reserve.
2. Steam asparagus spears for just a minute; cool and reserve.
3. Oil one oven-proof casserole dish large enough to contain the two chicken breasts.

ASSEMBLY
1. Lay the two chicken breasts in casserole dish. Top with two shrimp on each end of chicken. Add asparagus in center of shrimp. Dot with butter and nutmeg.
2. Lay one slice of Monterey Jack cheese on top of each shrimp and chicken. Garnish with parsley.
3. Bake in a preheated 400° oven for 25 minutes.
4. Remove from oven with spatula. Serve on heated plates.

2 whole chicken breasts, skinned, boned, halved and
    flattened with excess fat removed
2 very ripe pears, peeled, cored, quartered
4 slices Monterey Jack cheese
1/2 cup flavored bread crumbs
1/2 cup ginger ale
1 teaspoon brown sugar
1 teaspoon soy sauce
1/8 teaspoon ginger
1/2 cup chopped pecans
2 teaspoons butter
Sprig of chopped fresh parsley

PREPARATION
1. In a flat dish, press bread crumbs into chicken on both sides; reserve.
2. In a mixing bowl, mix ginger ale, brown sugar, soy sauce, ginger, pecans and parsley; reserve.
3. Oven-proof casserole dish large enough to contain the four chicken breasts.

ASSEMBLY
1. Place breaded chicken in casserole dish. Top chicken with half of pear. Top with Monterey Jack cheese and dot with butter.
2. Spoon ginger ale mixture around chicken.
3. Bake in a preheated 400° oven for 20 minutes.
4. Remove chicken to heated plates and spoon sauce around chicken.

THIS IS A GREAT DISH WHEN PEARS ARE IN SEASON.

PROVOLONE CHICKEN

2 whole chicken breasts, skinned, boned, halved and
    flattened with excess fat removed
4 slices provolone cheese
1/2 teaspoon oregano
1/2 cup flavored bread crumbs
Sprig of chopped parsley
2 teaspoons olive oil
1 teaspoon butter

PREPARATION
1. In a flat dish, press crumbs into chicken on both sides; reserve.
2. Oil one oven-proof casserole dish large enough to contain the
   four chicken breasts.

ASSEMBLY
1. Lay out breaded chicken in oiled casserole dish.
2. Sprinkle oregano on chicken. Top with provolone cheese.
   Garnish with parsley and dot with butter.
3. Bake in a preheated 400° oven for 20 minutes.
4. Remove from casserole with spatula. Serve on heated plates.

PEPPERONI CHICKEN

2 whole chicken breasts, skinned, boned,
   halved and flattened with excess fat removed
2 teaspoons olive oil
Sprig of chopped parsley
1/2 cup tomato sauce, (marinara sauce)
1/2 cup Ricotta cheese
20 thin slices pepperoni
2 teaspoons grated Parmesan cheese
4 slices provolone cheese

PREPARATION
1. In a flat dish, press crumbs into chicken on both sides; reserve.
2. Oil one oven-proof casserole dish large enough to contain the four chicken breasts.

ASSEMBLY
1. Lay chicken in oiled casserole dish. Top successively with 5 slices pepperoni, tomato sauce, Ricotta cheese, Parmesan cheese and provolone cheese. Garnish with chopped parsley.
2. Bake in a preheated 400° oven for 20 minutes.
3. Remove from oven with a spatula to hcatcd plates.

CHICKEN WITH FRESH APPLES AND MONTEREY JACK CHEESE

2 whole chicken breasts, skinned, boned
    halved and flattened with excess fat removed
2 apples
4 slices Monterey Jack cheese
1/2 cup flavored bread crumbs
Sprig of chopped parsley
1 cup cider or apple juice
Dash nutmeg
Dash paprika
2 teaspoons butter

PREPARATION
1. In a flat dish, press bread crumbs into chicken on both sides; reserve.
2. Peel apple, core, slice; reserve.
3. One oven-proof casserole dish large enough to contain the four chicken breasts.

ASSEMBLY
1. Lay chicken in casserole dish.
2. Top chicken with sliced apple. Add dash nutmeg. Top with Monterey Jack cheese. Top with parsley and paprika.
3. Add cider or apple juice to casserole and dot with butter.
4. Bake in a preheated 400° oven for 20 minutes.
5. Remove chicken to heated plates. Spoon sauce on chicken.

THIS DISH GOES WELL WITH RICE.

ARTICHOKE CHICKEN

2 whole chicken breasts, skinned, boned, halved and
    flattened with excess fat removed
1/2 cup flavored bread crumbs
1 package frozen artichokes, cooked according to
    directions, and drained or 1 small can of
    artichokes
1 cup chicken broth
4 slices Monterey Jack cheese
1/4 teaspoon sage
Sprig of chopped parsley

PREPARATION
1. In a flat dish, press bread crumbs into chicken on both sides; reserve.
2. Oven-proof casserole dish large enough to contain the four chicken breasts.

ASSEMBLY
1. Lay the chicken breasts in casserole dish. Top chicken with artichokes. Dust with sage. Top with Monterey Jack cheese. Garnish with parsley and dot with butter.
2. Add chicken broth to casserole.
3. Bake in a preheated 400° oven for 20 minutes.
4. Remove chicken to heated plates with a spatula. Spoon remaining juices around chicken.

2 whole chicken breasts, skinned, boned, halved and
 flattened with excess fat removed
2 oranges peeled and sliced with seeds removed
1/2 cup flavored bread crumbs
1/2 teaspoon grated orange rind
1 cup orange juice
1 teaspoon soy sauce
1 teaspoon brown sugar
1/4 teaspoon ginger
1/2 cup water
1/2 cup slivered or sliced almonds
1 small onion, chopped
2 teaspoons butter

PREPARATION

1. In a bowl, add orange juice, orange rind, soy sauce, brown sugar, water and chopped onion; reserve.
2. One oven-proof casserole dish large enough to contain the four breaded chicken breasts.

ASSEMBLY

1. Lay out chicken in casserole dish. Put orange slices on chicken. Top with almonds. Add orange juice mixture and dot with butter.
2. Bake in a preheated 400° oven for 20 minutes.
3. Remove chicken from casserole to heated plates and spoon remaining sauce on and around chicken.

THIS IS GREAT WITH RICE.

There is
no sight on earth
more appealing
than the
sight of a woman
making dinner
for someone
she
loves.

Thomas Wolfe

HONEY MUSTARD CHICKEN

2 whole chicken breasts, skinned, boned, halved and
    flattened with excess fat removed
2 teaspoons honey
3 teaspoons whole grain mustard
2 garlic cloves, chopped
Sprig fresh parsley
1/2 cup flavored bread crumbs
2 teaspoons olive oil
2 teaspoons butter

PREPARATION
1. In a flat dish, press bread crumbs into chicken on both sides;
   reserve.
2. In a bowl, mix together chopped garlic, mustard, honey,
   chopped parsley; reserve.
3. Oil one oven-proof casserole dish large enough to contain the
   four chicken breasts.

ASSEMBLY
1. Lay chicken in oiled casserole dish.
2. Spoon and spread the mustard mixture on breaded chicken.
3. Bake in a preheated 400° oven for 15 minutes.
4. Remove to heated plates. Spoon any remaining juices on
   chicken.

BROILED CHICKEN BREASTS

2 whole chicken breasts, skinned, boned, halved and
    flattened with excess fat removed
MARINADE:
1/2 cup olive oil
Juice of one lemon
2 teaspoons soy sauce
1/4 teaspoon basil
2 cloves chopped garlic
Pinch of fennel seeds

PREPARATION
1. In a mixing bowl, add olive oil, lemon juice, soy sauce, basil,
   chopped garlic and fennel. Mix well.
2. In a casserole dish large enough to contain the four chicken
   breasts, add chicken. Add marinade. Refrigerate chicken and
   turn three or four times for at least 2 hours.

ASSEMBLY
3. Preheat broiler and broil on both sides, 5 inches from broiler.
   Takes only about 5 minutes to cook. Don't over-cook.

ROLLED BACON AND MOZZARELLA CHICKEN

2 whole chicken breasts, skinned, boned, halved and
    flattened with excess fat removed
3 ounces whole milk mozzarella cheese, chopped
4 slices bacon, cooked and chopped
1/4 teaspoon basil
1 cup flavored bread crumbs
Sprig of fresh parsley, chopped
2 teaspoons olive oil
2 eggs
1/2 cup milk
1/2 cup flour for dredging
2 teaspoons butter
4 wooden toothpicks

PREPARATION

1. In a mixing bowl, add chopped mozzarella, chopped, cooked bacon, basil and chopped parsley. Mix well; reserve.
2. Oil an oven-proof casserole dish large enough to contain the four rolled chicken breasts.
3. In a mixing bowl, beat eggs and milk; reserve.
4. Add flour to a flat plate.
5. Add bread crumbs to a flat plate.

ASSEMBLY

1. On a flat surface, lay out chicken. Spoon cheese mixture in center of each chicken breast. Fold over cheese and roll like a jelly roll. Secure with a toothpick.
2. Dredge chicken rolls in flour, then egg mixture. Roll in bread crumbs.
3. Put chicken roll in oiled casserole dish and dot with butter.
4. Bake in a preheated 400° oven for 20 minutes.
5. Remove from oven to heated plates. To remove toothpicks, use needle-nose pliers and fork to hold chicken.

Cheese: Milk's leaps towards immortality

Clifton Fadiman

ROLLED CHICKEN WITH COCONUT

    2 whole chicken breasts, skinned, boned,
        halved and flattened with excess fat removed
    4 slices proscuitto or thinly sliced ham
    1 fresh ripe mango or fresh ripe peach
    1/2 cup flour for dredging
    1/2 teaspoon thyme
    1/8 teaspoon curry
    2 eggs
    1/2 cup milk
    1 cup unsweetened, grated coconut (available
        at natural food stores)
    2 teaspoons butter
    2 teaspoons olive oil
    4 large wooden toothpicks

PREPARATION
1. In a bowl, mix thyme, curry, flour; reserve.
2. In a bowl, beat eggs and milk together; reserve.
3. In a flat dish, add coconut; reserve.
4. Oil one oven-proof casserole dish large enough to contain the four rolled chicken breasts.

ASSEMBLY
1. On a flat surface, lay out flattened chicken breasts. Top with proscuitto or ham. Place mango or peach in center. Roll jelly roll style and secure with toothpicks.
2. Dredge chicken in flour mixture, then egg mixture. Roll in coconut coating completely.
3. Put chicken roll in oiled casserole dish and dot with butter.
4. Bake in a preheated 400° oven for 20 minutes.
5. Remove chicken from casserole to heated plates. Remove toothpicks, using needle-nose pliers to hold.

ROLLED CHICKEN WITH
BANANAS AND HAM

2 whole chicken breasts, skinned, boned, halved and
    flattened rather thin with excess fat removed
4 slices ham
2 ripe bananas
1 cup flavored bread crumbs
2 eggs
1/2 cup milk
1/2 cup flour
2 teaspoons olive oil
2 teaspoons butter
4 wooden toothpicks

PREPARATION
1. Oil an oven-proof casserole dish large enough to contain the
   four rolled chicken breasts.
2. In mixing bowl, beat eggs and milk; reserve.
3. Add flour to a flat plate.
4. Add bread crumbs to a flat plate.
5. Peel banana, cut in half, not split.

ASSEMBLY
1. On a flat surface, lay flattened chicken breasts. Top successively
   with ham, banana and chopped parsley. Roll like a jelly roll and
   secure with toothpicks.
2. Dredge rolled chicken in flour, then egg mixture. Roll in bread
   crumbs, coating completely.
3. Lay breaded chicken breasts in oiled casserole dish and dot with
   butter.
4. Bake in a preheated 400° oven for 20 minutes.
5. Remove chicken to heated plates. Remove toothpicks using
   needle-nose pliers and fork to hold.

DUTCH STYLE CHICKEN

2 whole chicken breasts, skinned, boned, halved
    and flattened rather thin with excess fat removed
4 pieces Gouda cheese, cubed into 1 inch strips,
1/2 inch thick, 1/2 inch wide
Sprig chopped parsley
1/2 cup flour
2 eggs
1/2 cup milk
1 cup flavored bread crumbs
2 teaspoons butter
2 teaspoons olive oil
4 wooden toothpicks

PREPARATION
1. Oil an oven-proof casserole dish large enough to contain the
four rolled chicken breasts.
2. In a mixing bowl, beat eggs and milk; reserve.
3. Add flour to a flat plate.
4. Add bread crumbs to a flat plate.

ASSEMBLY
1. On a flat surface, lay out flattened chicken breasts. Top in center
with Gouda cheese and parsley. Roll like a jelly roll and secure
with toothpicks.
2. Press rolled chicken in flour, then egg mixture. Roll in bread
crumbs; coating completely.
3. Lay breaded chicken in oiled casserole dish and dot with butter.
4. Bake in a preheated 400° oven for 20 minutes.
5. Remove chicken to heated plates. Remove toothpicks using
needle-nose pliers and fork to hold.

ROLLED CHICKEN AL D'AMICO

2 whole chicken breasts, skinned, boned, halved and
     flattened rather thin with excess fat removed
     1/2 teaspoon of fresh or dried rosemary
4 slices ham or proscuitto
4 slices provolone cheese
1/2 cup frozen peas
1 cup brown sauce (available at markets)
1 cup flavored bread crumbs
2 eggs
1/2 cup milk
4 large toothpicks
2 teaspoons butter
2 teaspoons olive oil
1/2 cup flour

PREPARATION
1. Oil an oven-proof casserole dish large enough to contain the four rolled chicken breasts.
2. In a mixing bowl, beat eggs and milk; reserve.
3. Add flour to a flat plate.
4. Add bread crumbs to a flat plate.

ASSEMBLY
1. On a flat surface, lay out flattened chicken breasts. Top successively with chopped rosemary, slice ham or prosciutto and provolone cheese. Roll like a jelly roll and secure with toothpicks.
2. Dredge rolled chicken in flour, then egg mixture. Roll in bread crumbs, coating completely.
3. Lay breaded chicken in oiled casserole dish and dot with butter.
4. Bake in a preheated 400° oven for 20 minutes.
5. Remove chicken to heated plates. Remove toothpicks using needle-nose pliers and fork to hold.

SAUCE
1. Make sure peas are thawed. Heat sauce. Add peas and spoon sauce on and around chicken.

THIS IS A RED ROOSTER FAVORITE FOR WEDDINGS.

NOTES

ORDER FORM

SEAFOOD EXPRESSIONS
by Normand J. Leclair

I'm proud to announce my second cookbook "SEAFOOD EXPRESSIONS".
A collection of 312 pages of idea's and recipes for entertaining and cooking
for yourself and your family. This new book is written in the same easy style
as "CHICKEN EXPRESSIONS".

To order this new cookbook send $13.50 post paid to:
SEAFOOD EXPRESSIONS
P.O. Box 356
NORTH KINGSTOWN, RI 02852

NAME _____

STREET _____

CITY_____ STATE _____ ZIP_____

RE-ORDER FORM

CHICKEN EXPRESSIONS
by **Normand J. Leclair**

This collection of recipes are festive, delicious and easy to prepare. They can be preassembled, ready to be whisked into the oven, and baked with no further attention. You can then delight your guests with wonderful food and share the evening with them. This cookbook offers 50 delicious boneless breast of chicken recipes.

IF YOU WISH TO ORDER ADDITIONAL COPIES OF CHICKEN EXPRESSIONS. PLEASE SEND $11.00 PER BOOK (POSTAGE AND HANDLING INCLUDED) TO:
CHICKEN EXPRESSIONS
P.O. BOX 356
NORTH KINGSTOWN, RI 02852

NAME _____

STREET _____

CITY _____ STATE _____ ZIP _____

NOTES

NOTES

NOTES

NOTES